Read for a Better World™

I0877856

PUPPIES

A First Look

ANNA ANDERHAGEN

GRL Consultant, Diane Craig, Certified Literacy Specialist

Lerner Publications ◆ Minneapolis

Educator Toolbox

Reading books is a great way for kids to express what they're interested in. Before reading this title, ask the reader these questions:

What do you think this book is about? Look at the cover for clues.

What do you already know about puppies?

What do you want to learn about puppies?

Let's Read Together

Encourage the reader to use the pictures to understand the text.

Point out when the reader successfully sounds out a word.

Praise the reader for recognizing sight words such as *are* and *they*.

TABLE OF CONTENTS

Puppies 4

You Connect! 21
STEM Snapshot 22
Photo Glossary 23
Learn More 23
Index 24

Puppies

Baby dogs are called puppies.

Puppies are born with their eyes and ears closed.

Their eyes and ears open at about two weeks old.

Moms keep their puppies warm.

Puppies drink their mom's milk.

When did you start to walk?

Puppies start to walk at about three weeks old.

Puppies take many naps. They need rest to grow stronger!

What do you do
to grow stronger?

Puppies love to play.
They learn to take turns.

Puppies play fight.

They like to chase and dig.

What do you like to do for fun?

When they are happy, puppies wag their tails.

Dogs can live for thirteen years or more.

A puppy can be your best friend!

You Connect!

Have you ever seen a puppy?

What is something you like about puppies?

Do you take turns when you play?

STEM Snapshot

Encourage students to think and ask questions like scientists. Ask the reader:

What is something you learned about puppies?

What is something you noticed about puppies in the pictures in this book?

What is something you still don't know about puppies?

Photo Glossary

dig

eyes

nap

tail

Learn More

Culliford, Amy. *Super Cute Puppies*. New York: Crabtree Publishing, 2023.

Geister-Jones, Sophie. *Dogs*. Minneapolis: Pop!, 2020.

Rathburn, Betsy. *Baby Dogs*. Minneapolis: Bellwether Media, 2022.

Index

drink, 9
ears, 6, 7
eyes, 6, 7
mom, 8, 9
rest, 12
wag, 18

Photo Acknowledgments

The images in this book are used with the permission of: © Orientgold/Shutterstock Images, pp. 4–5; © studio hoto/Shutterstock Images, p. 6; © Marina Olena/Shutterstock Images, pp. 7, 23 (top right); © Tiplyashina Evgeniya/Shutterstock Images, p. 8; © Anna Hoychuk/Shutterstock Images, p. 9; © Tara Lynn and Co/Shutterstock Images, pp. 10–11; © Ermolaev Alexander/Shutterstock Images, pp. 12–13, 16, 23 (bottom left); © anetapics/Shutterstock Images, pp. 14–15; © Sandra Huber/Shutterstock Images, p. 15; © SasaStock/Shutterstock Images, pp. 17, 23 (top left); © Natalia Duryagina/Shutterstock Images, pp. 18, 23 (bottom right); © Dmytro Zinkevych/Shutterstock Images, p. 19; © ANURAK PONGPATIMET/Shutterstock Images, p. 20.

Cover Photograph: © Eric Isselee/Shutterstock Images

Design Elements: © Mighty Media, Inc.

Lerner Publications Company
An imprint of Lerner Publishing Group, Inc.
241 First Avenue North
Minneapolis, MN 55401 USA

For reading levels and more information, look up this title at www.lernerbooks.com.

Main body text set in Mikado a Medium.
Typeface provided by Hannes von Doehren.

Library of Congress Cataloging-in-Publication Data

Names: Anderhagen, Anna, author.
Title: Puppies : a first look / Anna Anderhagen ; GRL Consultant, Diane Craig, Certified Literacy Specialist.
Description: Minneapolis : Lerner Publications, [2025] | Series: Read about baby animals (read for a better world) | Includes bibliographical references and index. | Audience: Ages 5–8 | Audience: Grades K–1 | Summary: "Puppies wag their tails when they are happy. They love to play. Adorable photographs and leveled text help readers learn more about baby dogs"—Provided by publisher.
Identifiers: LCCN 2023033623 (print) | LCCN 2023033624 (ebook) | ISBN 9798765626399 (lib. bbg.) | ISBN 9798765629512 (pbk.) | ISBN 9798765636725 (epub)
Subjects: LCSH: Puppies—Juvenile literature.
Classification: LCC SF426.5 .A53 2023 (print) | LCC SF426.5 (ebook) | DDC 636.7/07–dc23/eng/20231108

LC record available at https://lccn.loc.gov/2023033623
LC ebook record available at https://lccn.loc.gov/2023033624

Manufactured in the United States of America
1 - CG - 7/15/24